TO THE LEADER

First, thank you. Thanks for taking on the joy and the responsibility of leading a group through an important study of world religions and how Christians can think about and relate to people of other faiths. Your willingness to prepare and lead will be a blessing to the participants who will take this journey with you. You will also find blessings for yourself since, as the old adage goes, the best way to learn is to teach!

The study is based on the revised edition of Adam Hamilton's book *Christianity and World Religions: Questions We Ask About Other Faiths.* Rev. Hamilton is the senior pastor of Church of the Resurrection in Leawood, Kansas, one of the largest and fastest-growing United Methodist congregations in the United States. He has numerous books and publications to his name, and he has a reputation for tackling difficult issues with clarity, theological insight, biblical grounding, and a pastor's touch.

Adam has a boundless curiosity, and in this book he brings a sincere heart to the question of how Christians ought to think about other faiths. Why are there so many religions? What do they believe? And how does God view the two-thirds of the world's population who aren't Christian? Adam approaches other faiths with a deep desire to know them accurately and a respect for what we have to learn from them. He also shows how Christians can deepen their own faith through dialogue with other faiths.

As leader of this group, you will find the following lesson plans easy to use, with material sufficient for every session. In fact, you may have more than you need, so you can choose from the options in the "Learning Together" sections to tailor the study to your group and allotted time.

The study includes six sessions, and it makes use of the following components:

- The book *Christianity and World Religions: Questions We Ask About Other Faiths: Revised Edition,*
- the DVD that accompanies the study, and
- this Leader Guide.

Participants in the study should plan on bringing Bibles and the *Christianity and World Religions* book to each session. If possible, notify those interested in the study in advance of the first session. Make arrangements for them to get copies of the book so that they can read the introduction and chapter 1 before the first group meeting.

USING THIS GUIDE WITH YOUR GROUP

Because no two groups are alike, this guide has been designed to give you flexibility and choice in tailoring the sessions for your group. The session format is listed below. You may choose any or all of the activities, adapting them as you wish to meet the schedule and needs of your particular group.

The leader guide offers a basic session plan designed to be completed in a session of about 45 minutes in length. Select ahead of time which activities the group will do, for how long, and in what order. Depending on which activities you select, there may be special preparation needed. The leader is alerted in the session plan when advance preparation is needed.

SESSION FORMAT

Planning the Session
- Session Goals
- Scriptural Foundation
- Special Preparation

Getting Started
- Opening Activity
- Begin with Prayer

Learning Together
- Video Study and Discussion
- Book and Bible Study and Discussion

Wrapping Up

- Closing Activity
- Closing Prayer

HELPFUL HINTS

Preparing for the Session

- Pray for the leading of the Holy Spirit as you prepare for the study. Pray for discernment for yourself and for each member of the study group.
- Before each session, familiarize yourself with the content. Read the book chapter and make notes on important points or questions you may have.
- Depending on the length of time you have available for group meetings, you may or may not have time to do all the activities. Select the activities in advance that will work for your group time and interests.
- Choose the session elements you will use during the group session, including the specific discussion questions you plan to cover. Be prepared, however, to adjust the session as group members interact and as questions arise. Prepare carefully, but allow space and flexibility for the Holy Spirit to guide you and your group as you meet.
- Prepare the room where the group will meet so that the space will enhance the learning process. Ideally, group members should be seated around a table or in a circle so that all can see one another. Movable chairs are best because the group will sometimes be forming pairs or small groups for discussion. Special seating arrangements for some sessions are also suggested in the planning notes.
- Since this study uses a DVD, make arrangements to play this in your meeting space.
- Bring a supply of Bibles for those who forget to bring their own.
- For most sessions you will also need a whiteboard and markers, or an easel with large sheets of paper and markers. You will often see instructions for using a large sheet of paper to record responses and ideas from the group. Feel free to use a whiteboard instead, and adapt the instructions as necessary.

Shaping the Learning Environment

- Begin and end on time.
- Create a climate of openness, encouraging group members to participate as they feel comfortable.
- Remember that some people will jump right in with answers and comments, while others need time to process what is being discussed.
- If you notice that some group members seem never to be able to enter the conversation, ask them if they have thoughts to share. Give everyone a chance to talk, but keep the conversation moving. Moderate to prevent a few individuals from doing all the talking.
- Communicate the importance of group discussions and group exercises.
- If no one answers at first during discussions, do not be afraid of silence. Count silently to ten, then say something such as, "Would anyone like to go first?" If no one responds, venture an answer yourself and ask for comments.
- Model openness as you share with the group. Group members will follow your example. If you limit your sharing to a surface level, others will follow suit.
- Encourage multiple answers or responses before moving on.
- To help continue a discussion and give it greater depth, ask, "Why?" or "Why do you believe that?" or "Can you say more about that?"
- Affirm others' responses with comments such as "Great" or "Thanks" or "Good insight," especially if it's the first time someone has spoken during the group session.
- Monitor your own contributions. If you are doing most of the talking, back off so that you do not train the group to listen rather than speak up.
- Remember that you do not have all the answers. Your job is to keep the discussion going and encourage participation.

Managing the Session

- Honor the time schedule. If a session is running longer than expected, get consensus from the group before continuing beyond the agreed-upon ending time.
- Involve group members in various aspects of the group session, such as saying prayers or reading the Scripture.

- Note that the session guides sometimes call for breaking into smaller groups or pairs. This gives everyone a chance to speak and participate fully. Mix up the groups; don't let the same people pair up for every activity.
- As always in discussions that may involve personal sharing, confidentiality is essential. Group members should never pass along stories that have been shared in the group. Remind the group members at each session that confidentiality is crucial to the success of this study.

11

1

THE WISE MEN

PLANNING THE SESSION

Session Goals

As a result of conversations and activities connected with this session, group members should be able to:

- articulate the value of studying other religions as a means of understanding our neighbors;
- define what a theology of religions is and the questions it seeks to answer;
- identify three different perspectives on other religions: religious pluralism, Christian exclusivism, and Christian inclusivism; and
- point to biblical resources for understanding other religions.

Scriptural Foundation

After Jesus was born in Bethlehem in the territory of Judea during the rule of King Herod, magi came from the east to Jerusalem. They asked, "Where is the newborn king of the Jews? We've seen his star in the east, and we've come to honor him."...

[Herod] sent them to Bethlehem, saying, "Go and search carefully for the child...." They went; and look, the star they had seen in the east went ahead of them until it stood over

*the place where the child was. When they saw the star, they
were filled with joy. They entered the house and saw the child
with Mary his mother. Falling to their knees, they honored
him. Then they opened their treasure chests and presented
him with gifts of gold, frankincense, and myrrh.*

(Matthew 2:1-2, 8a, 9-11)

Special Preparation

- If the participants in your group are not familiar with one another, provide materials for name tags.
- Have Bibles available for those who may not bring them.
- Provide paper, pens, and pencils for participants.
- Provide a means for showing the DVD (e.g., TV/DVD player) and cue Session 1: The Wise Men.
- Arrange your seating in a circle or semicircle so that all participants can see one another.
- Prepare a large sheet of paper in the following way and post it in a visible location in your meeting area: First, write "A Theology of Religions Answers..." across the top of the sheet. Next, write the following questions from the study book below:
    - ◊ Why are there so many different religions?
    - ◊ What is the relationship between these religions?
    - ◊ How does God look at people of other religions?
    - ◊ What is the eternal fate of those who practice a religion other than the one I follow?
- Write "Why Study Other Religions?" at the top of a second large sheet of paper and post it in another visible area of the room.
- Have additional large sheets of blank paper and markers available.
- Find various objects (at least two) for a drawing exercise (take care that the objects are hidden from group members). The objects should be unusually shaped or textured. Read through the exercise titled "Draw an Object to Experience 'Feeling the Elephant'" below to visualize what might be needed. Two suggestions are a simple child's toy (e.g., a wooden horse) and a seashell.

GETTING STARTED

①ᵃ Opening Activity: Begin by Exploring Traditions

If your group members are not familiar with one another, invite them to put on a name tag as they enter. Once everyone is present and seated, ask the group to introduce themselves by name.

Now say: "Welcome to this study of *Christianity and World Religions*. One of the goals for this study is for us to understand our neighbors better. So let's begin by getting to know our neighbors in this group just a little bit better."

Ask group members to find a partner, preferably someone they do not know well, and move to a space in the room where they can talk. (This exercise can be done with both persons standing.) Tell each pair to identify which one will do the following exercise first. Now ask the person going first to talk for sixty seconds about what a typical meal in their childhood home looked like. What did you eat? Where did everyone sit? Were there certain rituals, like saying grace, that were observed?

During this first minute, the other partner should remain silent and listen. Then switch roles and have the second partner share their experiences of a meal in their childhood home. Set a timer so that you can signal when the sixty seconds are up.

Now have everyone come back to the larger group. Ask:

- What did you learn about your partner's household traditions?
- In what ways were your experiences different?
- How do our family traditions shape our expectations of what mealtime is supposed to look like?

Say: "In this study, we are going to encounter a number of different traditions that may challenge and enrich us. Let's pray that we will grow to love our neighbors and God more through these sessions together."

⟨149⟩ Begin with Prayer

Offer the following prayer or one of your own:

God of many nations,
we trust you
and we believe that your desire is for all people to know your love.

14

As we seek to know our neighbors better,
help us grow to love them more,
and to see your intentions for all creation. Amen.

LEARNING TOGETHER

Video Study and Discussion

In chapter 1, Adam Hamilton outlines the importance for Christians of developing a theology of religions, and he shares his hopes for this study. In the video, he offers some basic questions that Christians ask about other religions. He also presents three possible perspectives offered by Christians to the question of the fate of people of other religions: exclusivism, universalism or religious pluralism, and Christian inclusivism. The video also includes an interview with Matt and Sangeeta, an interfaith couple. See a transcript of this interview on page 16 under the heading "A Conversation About Faith."

Play the video segment for Session 1 and then discuss some of the following questions:

- What are Adam Hamilton's aims in putting together this study? Why is it important that we understand the two-thirds of the world's people who are not Christian?
- How often do you think about the questions that Adam Hamilton asks? How can they help us love our neighbors better?
- Matt and Sangeeta talk about the practices that have helped them live together as an interfaith couple. What are those practices? When has a conversation or a meal helped you understand someone with whom you felt you had little in common?

Book and Bible Study and Discussion

Consider People of Other Faiths

Invite participants to think about the people they interact with in the course of a normal weekday. Ask:

- How many of the people whom you meet are followers of a faith other than Christianity?
- How often is faith a subject that you have talked about with people of another faith?
- What things about their faith make you curious to know more?

A Conversation About Faith

Matt and Sangeeta attend the Church of the Resurrection. Matt grew up in the church. Sangeeta is from a Hindu family. They married several years ago, and Sangeeta attends worship with Matt while continuing to be a Hindu. They are learning how to be a married couple from two different religions. Here's an excerpt of an interview we conducted with them:

Sangeeta: What we talk about often is the centrality of ethics. "Love thy neighbor" is one example of that. But it's also in the Golden Rule, doing unto others as you would have done unto you.

Matt: What did Jesus do at the Last Supper? I think bringing together different faiths over food is such an integral thing in different communities. Once you start eating something different, you start hearing, "What is that?" And you start learning so much that you start becoming empathetic toward another person of another faith. And you start to see the world through their eyes—which I think opens you up to be more inclusive of all people.

Sangeeta: To really grasp where someone else is coming from, I think you have to be open to having conversations, to be loving in those conversations, and carefully try to understand where someone else has come from a deep place with their own beliefs and faith.

Matt: I think it goes back to stories, too—telling stories. Telling stories I think both humanizes and helps you relate to a different religion, a foreign culture. If we can't somehow get outside of our comfort zone as Christians and really live into what Jesus preaches, then we're going to have trouble talking to those billions of people. And I think that there's something about telling stories and eating food and just loving on one another—that's the way to talk to them as a Christian.

Say: "Adam Hamilton shares in his book that two-thirds of the world's population is not Christian, including 100 million Americans. He also states that his hope for this study is that we will understand our neighbors better."

As people respond to the following questions, write responses on the large sheet titled "Why Study Other Religions?" that you have posted prior to the session. Ask:

- Why should we study other religions?
- How is learning about people of other faiths a way of loving our neighbors?
- What are your hopes for this study?

Define a Theology of Religions

Read the section in chapter 1 about Grandfather Hamilton and a theology of religions (page 14). Invite group members to consider the messages about other religions they received in their family of origin. Ask participants to find a partner or two and discuss the following questions among themselves:

- Was the theology of religions in your family of origin closer to Grandfather Hamilton's or the man in Adam Hamilton's congregation? Or was it different from both?
- How has your understanding of other religions changed through your life?

After allowing some time for discussion, bring the whole group back together and direct their attention to the sheet you posted earlier titled "A Theology of Religions Answers..." Invite the group to read the questions on this sheet aloud in unison. Ask:

- Which of these questions seems most interesting to you? Why?
- What other questions have you had about other religions?

Read p unto

Recreate the Journey of the Magi

Invite a volunteer who is a good public reader to read Matthew 2:1-12 from the Bible as others follow along. Divide into small groups of three to four persons. Ask the groups to quickly scan the section of chapter 1 about the journey of the magi to visit Jesus (pages 23–24). Then ask them to discuss the passage from Matthew using the following guiding questions:

- Who are the magi?
- Why might God have included them in the story of Jesus' birth?
- What do we learn about God from their inclusion in the story?

After some time for discussion, come back together as a large group and share insights from the small groups.

Next, ask for four volunteers to do an improvisational sketch about the magi. Have one person play the role of a television journalist reporting live from the field as she or he interviews the three other volunteers playing the roles of magi. Have the journalist ask questions related to the discussion you have just done, asking the basics of Who? What? Where? When? and Why? Encourage the actors to have fun with the exercise and thank them when they have finished.

Now ask:

- What is something new you learned from revisiting the story of the magi?
- What is surprising about them?

Consider the Hidden God

Once again, direct attention to the sheet titled "A Theology of Religions Answers…." Have the group read the first question aloud. Now say: "Adam Hamilton explores this first question in the section of chapter 1 titled 'The Hidden God'" (pages 15–17). Ask:

- In what ways have you experienced God as hidden?
- What are some reasons why God chooses to be known indirectly?

Read aloud the story of Adam Hamilton's encounter with a physicist in the section "The Hidden God" (pages 16–17). Ask:

- How does Hamilton see God as something similar to the fundamental forces of nature?
- How does this understanding help to explain the existence of multiple religions?

Draw an Object to Experience "Feeling the Elephant"

Get the various objects you provided before the session, taking care not to let the other group members see the objects. Invite volunteers who will be guest artists. Assure the group that you are not looking for high-quality art.

Have the volunteers come to a table in pairs. Put a blank piece of paper and a drawing utensil in front of each.

Now ask the pair of volunteers to put their hands behind their backs with their palms upturned to receive an object. Tell them and the group that you will be placing an object in their hands for them to manipulate for a few seconds. They will then draw the object just from having felt it.

Stand behind the volunteers, choose one of the objects, and hold it up so that the group can see it. Then place the object in the hands of the first volunteer. Allow the volunteer to hold it for a few seconds, then move it to the second volunteer. Have the volunteers draw quickly their impressions of the object. After they finish, show the drawings to the group, then show the object to the volunteers.

If you have time, repeat the exercise with a different pair of volunteers and a different object. At the conclusion of the exercise, ask:

- How were the drawings similar?
- How were they different?
- How might this exercise help us understand the relationship between different religions?

Read the section of chapter 1 titled "Come Find Me" (pages 18–21). Ask:

- What is the incarnation?
- How does God's incarnation in Jesus help Christians understand who God is?

Study Different Perspectives on Religions

Divide into three groups. Assign each small group one of the three perspectives on religion that Hamilton defines in chapter 1: religious pluralism (or universalism), exclusivism, and Christian inclusivism. Ask the groups to study the section of chapter 1 that describes the perspective they have been assigned (see pages 25–29). Ask them to prepare a short report to the total group that answers the following questions:

- How does Hamilton define this perspective?
- How does this perspective view people of other faiths?
- What supports this perspective?

Have the groups prepare a large sheet of paper defining their perspective that they can post on the walls during their presentation.

Regather as a total group and have each group give a brief presentation on the perspective they have been assigned. Now read aloud the section at the conclusion of chapter 1 in which Hamilton quotes C. S. Lewis (page 30). Ask:

- What perspective does C. S. Lewis present in this passage?
- How is it an expression of God's mercy?

WRAPPING UP

Read the Closing of Jonah

Ask for three readers to read Jonah 3:10–4:11. Set the scene by saying that this is the end of the Book of Jonah and that the people of Nineveh, a non-Jewish city, have repented from their evil ways. Have one reader be the narrator. The other two readers should read the parts of Jonah and God.

After the reading, thank the volunteers and ask:

- How does this story reveal God's grace and mercy?
- What message might there be for us as we consider people of other religions?

Close with a Prayer

Close with the following prayer, or ask a group member to lead the group in a prayer of his or her own:

God, thank you for your abundant love to us that is anything but hidden. Thank you for coming in the person of Jesus to reveal yourself more fully to us. Help us to take the time in love to learn about our neighbors, to break bread with them and listen to their stories. Like the magi who saw your light and responded, let your light shine through us so the world can see. In Jesus' name, Amen.

2

HINDUISM

PLANNING THE SESSION

Session Goals

As a result of conversations and activities connected with this session, group members should be able to:

- identify the historical roots and sacred texts of Hinduism;
- articulate some of the basic beliefs of Hinduism;
- compare and contrast some Christian beliefs with those of Hinduism; and
- appreciate the possibilities and potential benefits of Christian-Hindu interactions.

Scriptural Foundation

At one time you were like a dead person because of the things you did wrong and your offenses against God. You used to live like people of this world. You followed the rule of a destructive spiritual power. This is the spirit of disobedience to God's will that is now at work in persons whose lives are characterized by disobedience. At one time you were like those persons. All of you used to do whatever felt good and whatever you thought you wanted so that you were children headed for punishment just like everyone else.

However, God is rich in mercy. He brought us to life with Christ while we were dead as a result of those things that we did wrong. He did this because of the great love that he has for us. You are saved by God's grace! And God raised us up and seated us in the heavens with Christ Jesus. God did this to show future generations the greatness of his grace by the goodness that God has shown us in Christ Jesus.

You are saved by God's grace because of your faith. This salvation is God's gift. It's not something you possessed. It's not something you did that you can be proud of. Instead, we are God's accomplishment, created in Christ Jesus to do good things. God planned for these good things to be the way that we live our lives.

(Ephesians 2:1-10)

Special Preparation

- Have Bibles available for those who may not bring them.
- Provide paper, pens, and pencils for participants.
- Provide a means for showing the DVD segment (e.g., TV/DVD player) and cue Session 2: Hinduism.
- Arrange your seating in a circle or semicircle so that all participants can see one another.
- Prepare a large sheet of paper with the following incomplete sentence as a heading: "When I think of Hinduism or people of the Hindu faith, I think of..." Post this paper in an accessible and visible place in the room.
- Have markers and additional large sheets of paper available.
- Prepare a group of index cards with the following definitions and post them on the wall in an accessible place in the room:
  ◊ Sacred scriptures of Hinduism
  ◊ Commentaries on the sacred scriptures
  ◊ Best-known sacred text among Hindus
  ◊ Charioteer/god in the best-known Hindu text
  ◊ Prince in the best-known Hindu text
  ◊ Most common name for the one god of Hinduism
  ◊ Name for the soul possessed by all creatures
  ◊ Duty to God
  ◊ Energy created by deeds

◊ Cycle of birth, life, death, rebirth
◊ Final release from reincarnation cycle
◊ Reunion with God
◊ Noninjury

- Get three packs of sticky notes, each of a different color. For each colored pack, write the following words, one word per sticky note, so that you have the full collection of words in three separate stacks. You will give each pack to one of three small groups:
  ◊ Ahimsa
  ◊ Arjuna
  ◊ Atman
  ◊ Bhagavad Gita
  ◊ Brahman
  ◊ Dharma
  ◊ Karma
  ◊ Krishna
  ◊ Moksha
  ◊ Nirvana
  ◊ Samsara
  ◊ Upanishads
  ◊ Vedas

- Prepare a large sheet of paper with the following heading: "Reincarnation and Salvation." Create a table with three columns and four rows, allowing plenty of room to write responses. In the top row, leave the first box blank and then write "Hinduism" in the second box and "Christianity" in the third box. In the second row of the first column, write "What Salvation Looks Like." In the third row write "What We Need to Be Saved From." In the fourth row write "Role of Good Works." Leave the other boxes blank. Post the sheet in a visible location.

GETTING STARTED

Opening Activity: Consider Associations with Hinduism

As participants arrive, have them choose a marker and write a response to the incomplete sentence ("When I think of Hinduism or people of the Hindu faith, I think of...") that you posted on a large sheet of paper prior to the session.

When the group has arrived, draw their attention to the paper and read aloud the responses that group members have written. Invite participants to share other responses that have not been written on the paper. Ask:

- How many of your associations with Hinduism were formed before reading chapter 2 in Hamilton's book?
- Where do your thoughts about Hinduism and people of the Hindu faith originate?
- How much do you interact with people of the Hindu faith? Have your interactions included talk about faith?

Say: "In this session we are going to be looking at some of the basic beliefs of Hinduism and looking at ways that those beliefs connect with and diverge from Christianity. Our goal is, as Adam Hamilton says, to be able better to love our neighbors and to understand our own faith."

Begin with Prayer

Offer the following prayer or one of your own:

God of all peoples,
You speak to us in many ways,
*   from the beauty of the world around us*
*   to the stories we receive from our ancestors in the faith*
*   and your revelation in Jesus Christ.*
It was Jesus who told us to love our neighbors
*   and we come together today to learn about our Hindu neighbors.*
Help us meet you in our meeting.
Amen.

LEARNING TOGETHER

Video Study and Discussion

In chapter 2, Adam Hamilton discusses Hinduism—its history, sacred texts, and beliefs, along with points of connections and divergence between Christian and Hindu beliefs. Using the examples of Gandhi and Martin Luther King Jr., he also shows how Christians and Hindus can learn from each other. In the video he recaps some of the major points of the chapter and includes parts of an interview he conducted with Dr. Debabrata "Deb" Bhaduri, a leader at the Hindu temple in Shawnee, Kansas. See a transcript of this interview on page 26 under the heading "Conversation with a Hindu."

Play the video segment for Session 2 and then discuss some of the following questions:

- Name some of the Hindu beliefs that are mentioned in this video. Which of them seems hardest to understand? Which make you want to know more?
- As Adam Hamilton interviews Dr. Deb Bhaduri, the video shows pictures of the Hindu temple where Dr. Bhaduri worships. What did you notice about this worship space and the worshipers?
- At the end of the video, Adam Hamilton challenges us to know our own faith well enough to enter into dialogue with people of other religions. How would you feel if a person of another faith came to interview you about what Christians believe?

Book and Bible Study and Discussion

Play a Matching Game with Words Related to Hinduism

Divide the group into three teams and give each team one of the stacks of sticky notes, which you prepared before the session. Say to the group: "In this session we learned a number of terms related to Hinduism. We're going to play a game to see how well we remember what those terms are."

Draw attention to the index cards you posted on the wall prior to the session. Say to the group: "These are the definitions for the Hindu terms on your cards. Your goal, without looking in the study book, is to match the terms with the correct definition. Place one of your team's sticky notes next to each definition."

Allow time for teams to discuss and post their sticky notes. Now read out the correct answers, commending groups that made the correct match. The list of correct responses is below:

- Sacred scriptures of Hinduism—*Vedas*
- Commentaries on the sacred scriptures—*Upanishads*
- Best-known sacred text among Hindus—*Bhagavad Gita*
- Charioteer/god in the best-known Hindu Text—*Krishna*
- Prince in the best-known Hindu text—*Arjuna*
- Most common name for the one god of Hinduism—*Brahman*
- Name for the soul possessed by all creatures—*Atman*
- Duty to God—*Dharma*
- Energy created by deeds—*Karma*
- Cycle of birth, life, death, rebirth—*Samsara*

CONVERSATION WITH A HINDU

To get a better sense of what Hindus believe—and where Christians might find places of both agreement and disagreement—I think it makes sense to hear directly from a Hindu. So in preparing for my sermon on Hinduism and Christianity, and for this this book, I talked with Dr. Debabrata Bhaduri, a leader at the Hindu temple in Shawnee, Kansas. Dr. Bhaduri, a nuclear physicist by training, has devoted his career to the area of oncology, working at Kansas University and then at Veterans' Medical Center. But his passion is his faith. I asked him to summarize the major tenets of his faith. Here is an excerpt from our conversation:

Central to Hindu religion is that there is an almighty, supreme God, which is in the whole universe as well as in every soul. And it is our duty to realize that soul by means of various rituals and practices. Of course, meditation is one of the higher stages of that realization. The supreme God, which we call Brahman, is the source of the deities. And we have many deities in Hinduism, but they are manifestations of that supreme God, a certain aspect of God.

We believe that every person has a soul. We call it the self. The soul inhabits the body and lives in this life, and then when this life ends the body is destroyed, but the soul does not get destroyed. It transmigrates to another life, another person is born, or maybe another animal is born, and then that soul goes to that body, and then is another life. So in this way the soul is everlasting.

In that lifetime the work, or the karma (karma means the way you work or behave in the world), actually determines your fate in the next life. And so people who have done good karma will be born into a better condition, a better life. And in this way Hindus believe that the life is always evolving in that sense, by doing more and more good actions.

But our main goal is to pray to God or connect to God. And then we do our duties toward the family, for the society, for the nation; all these things are described in the Hindu guidelines. And by doing all these things I try to perfect my soul more and more.

- Final release from reincarnation cycle—*Moksha*
- Reunion with God—*Nirvana*
- Noninjury—*Ahimsa*

Explore the Hindu Understanding of God

Invite participants to reflect on a time when they felt close to God. Some potential responses might be a worship service when they felt God speak to them, an experience of God in a beautiful natural setting, or the birth of a child. After volunteers have a chance to share briefly, ask:

- What does it mean to you that God is personal?
- How do you understand God's presence at times when you are unaware of God's presence?

Read aloud (or have a volunteer read) the section of chapter 2 titled "One Transpersonal God but Multiple Deities" (pages 37–39). Ask:

- How did Adam Hamilton react when he was offered an apple at the Hindu temple?
- Would you have eaten the apple if you had been there? Why or why not?
- What is the difference between believing that God is personal and believing that God is beyond personal?

Depict the Hindu Belief in Reincarnation

Divide into small groups of two to three people. Distribute one large sheet of paper to each small group along with markers. Ask the group to review the section of chapter 2 titled "Every Creature Has a Soul That Is Reincarnated" (pages 39–40). Invite them to discuss how Hinduism depicts the journey of the soul through life, death, and reincarnation. Ask them to consider these questions in their discussion:

- According to Hindu beliefs, what is the origin of the soul?
- What is the soul's duty to God?
- Why do humans do bad things?
- What is the significance of karma?
- What is the end of the cycle?

27

After allowing some time for discussion, invite the groups to draw the cycle of reincarnation on the paper. Encourage them to use their creativity in depicting the stages of the belief system.

Have each group present its drawing to the total group. Post the drawings on the wall, then gather the full group back together to share the drawings and discuss what you learned. Ask:

- What does the idea of reincarnation suggest about the Hindu worldview?

Study Ephesians

Invite participants to find Ephesians 2:1-10 in their Bibles. An excerpt of this passage is also found at the beginning of chapter 2 in the book. Say to the group: "Now that we have looked at Hindu beliefs about reincarnation, we are going to look at how Christians view some of the same questions. In Ephesians, Paul talks about how Christ offers salvation."

Invite a good reader to read Ephesians 2:1-10 aloud. Next, ask group members to read the passage again silently, making note of all the places in the passage where God acts.

Discuss the following questions as a group:

- According to this passage, what is the problem that plagues human beings?
- How does God "make us alive"?
- What is the role of our actions if salvation is the gift of God (verse 8)?

Now ask group members to scan the section of chapter 2 titled "Reincarnation and Salvation" (pages 44–47). Direct attention to the sheet you posted earlier titled "Reincarnation and Salvation." Based on their reading of this section, ask the group to compare Hinduism and Christianity in the categories listed in the first column of your prepared sheet. Write responses on the sheet in the appropriate places.

Discuss the Concept of Ahimsa

Read aloud the section of chapter 2 titled "Nonviolence: Ahimsa" (pages 40–41). Discuss the following questions:

- According to Adam Hamilton, how does Hinduism understand the obligation of "noninjury"?

- What are some of the ways that Hindus live out ahimsa in their lives?

Now invite group members to consider how Christianity approaches the question of nonviolence. Ask:

- What are some biblical passages that refer to nonviolence? (e.g., prophecy about turning swords into plowshares; Jesus' command to turn the other cheek; Jesus submitting to the violence of the cross, etc.)
- How have Christians practiced nonviolence?
- How do Hindu and Christian understandings of nonviolence converge and diverge?

Envision Learning from Each Other

Read aloud the section of chapter 2 titled "Learning from Each Other" (pages 48–49). Ask the group:

- What did Gandhi learn from Christianity?
- What did Martin Luther King Jr. learn from Gandhi?
- How are Gandhi and King models for how Hindus and Christians can learn from each other?

Invite group members to consider relationships they may already have with people of the Hindu religion or resources they have for learning more about Hinduism. Ask:

- How does Adam Hamilton suggest that we enter into conversations with our Hindu neighbors?
- What areas of Hinduism would you want to explore more?
- What do you imagine to be the benefits of continued dialogue?

WRAPPING UP

Return to the Associations Page

Direct the group's attention to the sheet of associations you developed at the beginning of the session (see "Getting Started"). Ask group members:

- Which of these impressions of Hinduism would you like to change based on this session?

- What new impressions would you like to add?

Offer a Time of Mutual Invitation

Explain to the group: Mutual invitation is a process that allows group members to share their thoughts about a particular question. In this process, I will begin and share my response to the question: "What have you learned about Hinduism that you want to keep as a blessing?"

After I share, I will invite one of you to share your own response to the same question. If you are ready to share, you may do so, or you may say, "I would like to pass for now." If you would not like to share at all, you may say, "I pass." But either way, please invite someone else to share.

We will continue until everyone has had a chance to share or pass. We will not be discussing or evaluating one another's responses, but simply sharing and listening.

Following these instructions, begin the sharing yourself and invite someone else to respond. Make sure that everyone has been invited and that you have returned to those people who indicated they would like to pass for now.

Close with a Prayer

Close the session by reading the following prayer, or offer a prayer of your own:

O God, we are grateful for your love, mercy, and grace. We are grateful that you are personal—that you know us, love us, and care for us more than we could possibly imagine. We are grateful that you came to us in Jesus Christ, born into this world, taking on human flesh and human feelings, living, growing, teaching, showing, suffering, dying, and rising. Help us to know who you are and who you call us to be. Thank you for our Hindu neighbors and friends. We pray that you might make us a blessing to them. Help us to listen and learn, and in the process grow in our own faith even as we encourage others and love them well. In your holy name. Amen.

3

BUDDHISM

PLANNING THE SESSION

Session Goals

As a result of conversations and activities connected with this session, group members should begin to:

- identify the historical roots and sacred texts of Buddhism;
- articulate some of the basic beliefs of Buddhism;
- compare and contrast some Christian beliefs with those of Buddhism; and
- appreciate the possible benefits of Christian-Buddhist interactions.

Scriptural Foundation

We also boast in our sufferings, knowing that suffering produces endurance, and endurance produces character, and character produces hope, and hope does not disappoint us, because God's love has been poured into our hearts through the Holy Spirit that has been given to us.

(Romans 5:3b-5, NRSV)

Special Preparation

- Provide Bibles for those who may not bring them.
- Have available paper, pens, and pencils for participants.

- Arrange your seating in a circle or semicircle so that all participants can see one another.
- Provide a means for showing the DVD segment (e.g., TV/DVD player) and cue Session 3: Buddhism.
- In your preparation time, reflect on a time in your life when you had to overcome some obstacle through significant struggle. Prepare a three-minute story about that period of your life to share with the group. Be sure to identify what the struggle involved and how you look back on it now.
- Post 2 large sheets of blank paper in accessible and visible locations on the wall.
- Provide markers and other large sheets of blank paper.
- Write the following heading on a large sheet of paper: "The Four Noble Truths of Buddhism." Beneath this heading write the four noble truths as they are found in the section in chapter 3 titled "Essential Buddhist Teachings" (page 58):
  1. Suffering is an integral part of life.
  2. Suffering results from attachments and desires.
  3. We can overcome suffering by overcoming our attachments.
  4. Following the Holy Eightfold Path is the way to find release from suffering.
- Write the following heading on another large sheet of paper: "Beliefs about Suffering." Post the sheet in an accessible location in the room.
- Bring a small bell or some other instrument for gently ending the silence in the "Wrapping Up" section.

GETTING STARTED

Opening Activity: Share Stories of Struggle

After group members have arrived, say: "In this session we are going to be talking about Buddhism, some of its central beliefs, and how Christians look at some of those same questions. One area that Adam Hamilton explores in his book is the role of suffering in human life. We all have stories of suffering. Let me tell you one of mine."

Relate to the group the story you prepared ahead of time (see "Special Preparation"). Share with participants how you think about the suffering that was a part of your story. How did the suffering affect the outcome of your story? In what ways was it hurtful? How was it helpful?

Now invite participants to reflect on a similar moment in their own lives when they overcame an obstacle through struggle. Ask them to evaluate the role that suffering played in shaping their story.

Ask group members to find a partner and share their stories with one another. Ask that each person take 90 seconds to tell their story. The other person in the pair should just listen as his or her partner shares. After 90 seconds give a signal to indicate that the listening person should now share his or her story. Offer a final period of 2 minutes for persons to share their reflections with each other on the role of suffering in their stories.

Begin with Prayer

Offer the following prayer or one of your own:

God of love,
in Jesus Christ you walked the paths we walk
and knew the suffering of this world.
You tell us that you are present with us in every situation.
We seek to love like you love
and to walk with others in their struggles.
Help us to grow in our time together
to love our neighbors more. Amen.

LEARNING TOGETHER

Video Study and Discussion

In chapter 3, Adam Hamilton discusses Buddhism from its history in the story of Siddhartha Gautama (the Buddha) to its central beliefs. In the video, Hamilton reviews highlights from the book and talks about key differences between Christianity and Buddhism. He also interviews Pete Potts, the executive director of the Inner Peace Buddhist Center in Kansas City, Missouri. See a transcript of this interview on page 34 under the heading "Conversation with a Buddhist."

Play the video segment for this chapter and then discuss some of the following questions:

- Pete Potts talks about the Buddhist idea of suffering or anxiety as "not-quite-rightness." How does that description compare with your understanding of suffering? What word or words would you use to describe "not-quite-rightness"? What more would you want to say about it?

- What are the major differences in how Christians and Buddhists think about the afterlife?
- Adam Hamilton says that one of the things he learned from Buddhism is an emphasis on "holding life loosely." How could this approach help us trust God more?

CONVERSATION WITH A BUDDHIST

Pete Potts grew up Lutheran, became a Buddhist as an adult, and was ordained a Tibetan Buddhist minister. Now she is the executive director of the Inner Peace Buddhist Center in Kansas City, Missouri. As I sat at the center one evening, I asked her to tell me about Buddhism's Four Noble Truths, and here is an excerpt from our interview.

The first Noble Truth is that life inherently has some stress; it's often interpreted as suffering. That's where Buddhism gets a bad name as being a big old downer. But [this first truth involves] the word *dukha*, which is hard to translate. *Dukha*... it's stressfulness. It's not-quite-rightness. And that's an inherent quality of life.

The Second Noble Truth is that that *dukha*, that stressfulness, that not-quite-rightness, is caused by clinging and craving and the attachments caused by that clinging craving.

The Third Noble Truth is that it is possible to relieve that suffering, relieve that not-quite-rightness. It's possible to stop that attachment.

And the Fourth Noble Truth is that there is an Eightfold Path. And if you practice and study and put into your life this Eightfold Path that you will begin to see the effects of reducing your attachment and your craving, and, therefore, you will reduce your suffering. The Eightfold Path is wise view, wise intention, wise speech, wise action, wise livelihood, wise effort, wise mindfulness, and wise concentration.

Or, to keep it pretty simple: Do as much good as you can. Refrain from doing evil, purify your mind.

Book and Bible Study and Discussion

Study Scripture

Ask group members to turn in a Bible to Romans 5:3-5. Have a volunteer take a marker and move to a large sheet of paper that you posted on the wall prior to the session. Invite another volunteer to read the passage slowly as other participants listen. Then have the volunteer read it again, pausing to note the nouns used. Ask the volunteer at the large sheet of paper to write each noun in large letters. Where the text talks about one noun producing something else (e.g., "Suffering produces endurance"), draw an arrow between the nouns.

After the second reading, direct attention to the words that you have written down. Ask:

- What noun begins this passage?
- What does this say about Paul's view of suffering?
- How does suffering relate to God's love?
- What questions would you want to ask Paul about suffering in the Christian life?
- How could this passage be comforting in the midst of suffering?

Explore the Story of the Buddha

Divide into three small groups for this next exercise. Distribute large sheets of paper and markers to each group. Say to the participants: "Adam Hamilton tells us the story of the Buddha in the opening sections of chapter 3. Each of the groups is going to explore a different part of that story and report back to the larger group. Feel free to use your creativity in your presentations."

Assign each group one of the following sections from chapter 3 to study: "The Story of the Buddha" (pages 53–55), "The Burden of Reality" (pages 55–56), and "The Awakening" (pages 56–57). Ask them to draw or write something related to this section on the sheet of paper they have been given and to prepare to present their part of the story to the large group. Use the following questions as a guide:

- What was going on in this part of Siddhartha Gautama's life?
- How did he respond to his discomfort?
- What was the result?

Allow some time for the small groups to work, then come back together for the presentations. After each group has had an opportunity to present, ask:

- When have you experienced some of the same feelings that Siddhartha did?
- How do most of us cope with the kind of anxiety Siddhartha experienced?
- What did you learn from his story?

Identify the Four Noble Truths

Direct the group's attention to the sheet of paper you prepared before the session that lists the Four Noble Truths of Buddhism. Remind participants that these four truths can also be found in the section of chapter 3 titled "Essential Buddhist Teachings" (page 58). Have the group read the four truths aloud in unison.

Ask the following questions. Invite group members to use the study book to help in answering:

- What are the attachments that the truths refer to?
- How can suffering result from attachments?
- In what ways does this understanding of suffering differ from what you believe?

Consider Christian Understandings of Suffering

Say to the group: "In the section of chapter 3 titled 'The Origin of and Solution to Suffering,' Adam Hamilton compares Christian and Buddhist beliefs about suffering. Let's spend a few minutes considering the differences between them."

Ask a volunteer to begin a chart on the large sheet of blank paper you posted before the session with the heading "Beliefs about Suffering." Have the volunteer draw a line down the center of the paper. As the group discusses the questions below, ask the volunteer to place Christian beliefs in one column and Buddhist beliefs in the other.

Ask the group to skim the section of chapter 3 titled "The Origin of and Solution to Suffering" (pages 62–65). Discuss the following questions as a group:

- How do Christianity and Buddhism view the primary human condition?

- What is the largest cause of suffering according to each faith?
- What is the answer to suffering according to each?
- How do Christians understand repentance and reconciliation?

Describe a Personal God

Ask group members to turn in a Bible to Psalm 23. Say to the group: "Psalm 23 is one of the most beloved passages in the Bible for Christians. It outlines a personal relationship with God."

Invite a volunteer with a good reading voice to read Psalm 23 aloud. Then have the participants read through the psalm again silently, noting images and words that describe the relationship of the psalmist to God. Ask:

- What are some of the images that speak most powerfully to you in this psalm?
- How would you describe the relationship between the psalmist and God?
- What does this suggest about how Christians view God?

Now read aloud the section of chapter 3 titled "God's Place in Our Lives" (page 67). Ask:

- What is the difference between Christian and Buddhist beliefs about God?
- How does faith in God help Christians approach the reality of suffering?

Examine the Eightfold Path and the Three General Rules

Read aloud the practices that form the Holy Eightfold Path (pages 58–59) and invite members also to recall the interview with Pete Potts in the video. Ask:

- How does Pete Potts summarize the Eightfold Path of Buddhism?

Have a volunteer write Potts's summary of the Eightfold Path on a blank sheet of paper posted in an accessible and visible spot on the wall, using numbers for each of the points:

1. Do as much good as you can.
2. Refrain from doing evil.
3. Purify your mind.

Next, have the volunteer write Adam Hamilton's summary of John Wesley's Three General Rules on the same sheet of paper:

1. Refrain from doing evil.
2. Do all the good you can.
3. Pursue the spiritual disciplines that help you stay and grow in love with God.

Discuss the following questions:

- What is the same in both of these summaries?
- What is different?
- How do the differences between the third points help us to understand the differences between Christianity and Buddhism?
- What do these lists suggest about the potential of Christians and Buddhists to work together in certain areas?

WRAPPING UP

Share God-moments

Ask group members to skim the section of chapter 3 titled "Appreciating Buddhism" (pages 68–71). Discuss the following questions as a group:

- What does Adam Hamilton appreciate about the Buddhist emphasis on mindfulness?
- What does he call moments when he is paying attention to what is happening around him?
- How did God show up for Hamilton in the examples that he gives?

Invite group members into a few minutes of silent reflection. Ask them to get into a comfortable sitting position with their legs and arms uncrossed. Have participants close their eyes and concentrate on their breathing. Ask them to quiet their bodies and minds and pay attention to how their body feels and what the room feels like. Ask them to be aware of how God is present in this moment.

After several minutes, gently bring persons back to the group, perhaps by chiming a small bell. Ask volunteers to share a word or phrase that expresses something about how they feel in this moment. Offer a short prayer of thanksgiving to God for God's presence.

Close with a Prayer

Close with the following prayer, or offer one of your own.

God, I lay before you my burdens and concerns. I ask you to give me peace. Comfort those who are struggling right now, and let them feel your presence. Help me to trust in you, to trust that you are always with me, and to trust in your love. Help me to feel your arms holding me and embracing me when I'm afraid. Help me to know that suffering will never have the final word. And help me to pay attention to what you may be doing in this world, and how I can be part of it. In Jesus' name. Amen.

4

JUDAISM

PLANNING THE SESSION

Session Goals

As a result of conversations and activities connected with this session, group members should begin to:

- identify the historical roots and sacred texts of Judaism;
- articulate some of the basic beliefs of Judaism;
- understand Christianity's origins in Judaism and continuing connection with it; and
- appreciate the possibilities of Jewish-Christian interactions.

Scriptural Foundation

> The LORD said to Abram, "Leave your land, your family, and your father's household for the land that I will show you. I will make of you a great nation and will bless you. I will make your name respected, and you will be a blessing.
>
> I will bless those who bless you,
>   those who curse you I will curse;
>   all the families of the earth
>   will be blessed because of you."
>
> *(Genesis 12:1-3)*

Special Preparation

- Have Bibles available for those who may not bring them.
- Provide paper, pens, and pencils for participants.
- Arrange your seating in a circle or semicircle so that all participants can see one another.
- Provide a means for showing the DVD segment (e.g., TV/DVD player) and cue Session 4: Judaism.
- Have additional sheets of blank paper available along with markers.
- Have enough blank index cards available to give eight to each pair of group members for the "Memorize Key Terms in Judaism" exercise and an additional blank card to each member for the "Wrapping Up" exercise.
- On a large sheet of paper, write the heading "Key Terms in Judaism." Under the heading write the following terms:
  ◊ Tanakh
  ◊ Torah
  ◊ Nevi'im
  ◊ Ketuvim
  ◊ Talmud
  ◊ Orthodox
  ◊ Conservative
  ◊ Reform
- On another large sheet of paper, write the heading "Understanding the Messiah." Post it in a visible and accessible place in the meeting area.

GETTING STARTED

Opening Activity: Tell Origin Stories

After participants have arrived, invite them to recall their families of origin and the place in which they spent their childhoods. Distribute blank pieces of paper and writing instruments. Ask group members to write down values that they grew up with that helped to shape them. Consider the following questions:

- What were things in my family or home community that helped me understand what it meant to be a responsible person?
- What was important to my family or community?

41

- What parts of my life today make no sense without understanding where I came from?

After giving persons time to work individually, invite volunteers to share some of their reflections briefly.

Now say to the group: "As Christians, we look to Judaism in much the same way that we have talked about our families and home communities. There are things about the Christian life that are impossible to understand without understanding Christianity's origins in Judaism."

Ask:

- What examples does Adam Hamilton give in his book of elements of Judaism that Christians share?
- How is studying Judaism different for Christians than studying Hinduism or Buddhism?

Begin with Prayer

Offer the following prayer or one of your own:

God of Abraham and Sarah,
we know your name because you have made yourself known
by the people you called.
God of Israel,
we trust you because you have bound yourself to a people.
God of Jesus Christ,
born of Mary as part of your covenant people,
we want to love our Jewish neighbors more.
Be with us here and now and help us grow in love. Amen.

LEARNING TOGETHER

Video Study and Discussion

In chapter 4, Adam Hamilton discusses Judaism—its history, sacred texts, branches, and beliefs. In the video he recaps some of the major points of the chapter and includes parts of an interview he conducted with Rabbi Art Nemitoff. See a transcript of this interview on page 43 under the heading "Conversation with a Rabbi."

Play the video segment for this chapter and then discuss some of the following questions:

- Adam Hamilton uses Genesis 12:1-4 to remind us of the blessing God gave to Abraham and Sarah. (Read these verses aloud.) What did God promise? What does it mean that Abraham and Sarah's descendants were to be a blessing to the nations?
- Rabbi Nemitoff talks about two central Jewish beliefs. What are they? (Belief in one God and a form of the Golden Rule.) If someone were to ask you what the central beliefs of Christianity are, what would you say?
- Rabbi Nemitoff describes the concept of a "world to come" as part of Jewish beliefs about the afterlife. How might this be like the kingdom Christians pray for in the Lord's Prayer? How might it be different?
- The video shows images from worship and community life in a Jewish synagogue. What impressions do you get from these brief clips about the nature of Jewish religious life? What things seemed

CONVERSATION WITH A RABBI

The oldest Jewish synagogue in Kansas City is Temple B'nai Jehudah. It goes back to 1870. In preparing this book, I went to visit with their senior rabbi, Art Nemitoff, who is a good friend of mine. I asked him to summarize for Christian readers what it means to be a Jew. What are the essential beliefs and practices? This is what he had to say:

There are two answers. One would be to quote the Book of Deuteronomy and to state the Shema, the watchword of our faith: "Sh'ma Yisra'eil Eloheinu Adonai Echad" (Hear, O Israel, the Lord our God, the Lord is One). While we do not have creeds in Judaism, as some faith traditions have, we do have this statement of belief. So that belief in one God is one essential, one way of describing Judaism.

The other is one of my favorite statements. It's a story told of Rabbi Hillel two thousand years ago. When challenged to explain what Judaism was all about, he said simply, "Do not do unto others what you would have them not do unto you. All the rest is commentary. Go and learn." It's basically the golden rule in reverse. And all the rest is how you make it in life.

familiar to you? What things seemed unusual or distinctive? What makes you want to know more?

Book and Bible Study and Discussion

Explore Anti-Semitism

Ask for a volunteer who has some drawing ability. Give the volunteer a large sheet of paper and some markers. Ask the rest of the group to close their eyes, and explain that you are going to describe a landscape. Have the volunteer draw the landscape as she or he imagines it while you describe it.

Say to the group: "Imagine a garden that has grown fertile plants for many years. In the middle of the field is a young tree that has been cared for by the gardener. The tree is not tall, but it is flourishing and growing.

"Now imagine that someone has come into the field with seeds of an invasive plant. The plant has long roots that choke out other plants that might be planted in the field. The planter has come back to water and cultivate the invasive plants so that they have grown into ugly, thorny bushes. These bushes surround the tree and mar the beauty of the field."

Now have the group members open their eyes. Invite the volunteer to share his or her sketch of the imagined landscape. Ask:

- What do you appreciate about our artist's rendition of the landscape?
- How would you describe this landscape?
- What is the problem that needs to be addressed?

Say to the group: "In the first section of chapter 4, Adam Hamilton describes some of the sad history of anti-Semitism. Take a minute to skim this opening section and identify some of the anti-Semitic incidents Hamilton describes."

After allowing some time for skimming the study book, invite participants to call out some of the incidents they found. Examples could include the Holocaust, expulsions, pogroms, restrictive covenants, the Kansas City shootings, or the Charlottesville alt-right march. As persons call out incidents, write the name of each over one of the invasive plants that your volunteer artist has drawn.

Say to the group: "Adam Hamilton compares anti-Semitism to a poisonous seed that has been 'watered and cultivated by misunderstanding and bad theology.'"

Discuss the following questions:

- What are some examples of misunderstanding between Christians and Jews?
- Why is anti-Semitism a perversion of our faith values?

Post the drawing on the wall in a visible and accessible location.

Study Scripture Related to Christianity's Roots in Judaism

Have participants turn in their Bibles to Romans 11:16-27. Ask a good reader to read the passage aloud slowly. Say to the group: "In this passage, the Apostle Paul is talking to Gentile (non-Jewish) Christians in an environment where there was conflict and misunderstanding between Christians and Jews. Paul is trying to explain the relationship between Christians and Jews, whom God has claimed as God's own people."

Discuss the following questions:

- What image does Paul use to describe the relationship between Jews and Christians?
- Looking at the tree in our drawing once again, what part of the tree represents the Jewish people?
- What part would represent Christians?

Ask your volunteer artist to label the trunk of the tree "Judaism." Then label a branch of the tree "Christianity"

Next have participants turn their Bibles to Mark 12:28-31. Ask another volunteer to read this passage aloud. Say: "On pages 88–89 of his book, Adam Hamilton identifies the Shema and the Golden Rule as the first two key beliefs of Judaism." Ask:

- How do these key beliefs compare with Jesus' response about the greatest commandment?
- What do these two passages, Romans 11:16-27 and Mark 12:28-31, suggest to you about the relationship between Christianity and Judaism?
- How is our relationship to Judaism different from our relationship with other faiths, such as Hinduism and Buddhism?

Memorize Key Terms in Judaism

Have participants divide into pairs for the next activity. Distribute eight blank index cards to each pair. Have one person from each pair write down the eight words from the "Key Terms" sheet you posted before the session began—one word on each card.

Now ask the pair to skim through chapter 4 to find a definition for each term. Write each definition on the back of the appropriate card.

After allowing some minutes for this activity, ask the pair to use their prepared cards as flash cards for memorization. Have one person in each pair hold up the definition while the other person tries to give the appropriate word. After the first person has a chance to run through the cards, switch and allow the other partner to repeat the exercise.

When pairs have had a chance to run through the exercise, ask a volunteer pair to stand in front of the group and do the exercise while others watch.

Discuss the following questions:

- How does the Talmud relate to the Tanakh?
- How are the branches of Judaism similar to branches of Christianity?
- What did these terms teach you about the relationship between Judaism and Christianity?

Discuss Atoning Sacrifice

Review the section of chapter 4 titled "Atoning Sacrifice" (page 90). Have a volunteer read this section aloud. Ask:

- How did the Jewish practice of animal sacrifice change after the destruction of the Temple in AD 70?
- What is the "sacrifice of the heart"?

Read aloud Psalm 51:15-17. Ask:

- What kind of sacrifice does the psalmist believe that God wants?
- How is this understanding of sacrifice important to Jews and Christians?

Consider the Place of Jesus as Messiah

Review the section of chapter 4 titled "Jesus as Messiah" (pages 93–94). Say to the group: "One of the fundamental differences between Jews and Christians concerns their beliefs about the Messiah. In this section of chapter 4, Adam Hamilton describes the differences in how each group views the Messiah."

Direct the group's attention to the blank sheet of paper you posted earlier titled "Understanding the Messiah." Under that heading draw two columns. Ask the group to describe the Messiah that Jewish people expected in the time of Jesus, based on Hamilton's description. Write responses in the left-hand column.

Now ask the group to describe the Messiah that Jesus' Jewish followers understood that they had seen in him. Write these responses in the right-hand column.

Ask:

- Why is it important to Christians that Jesus is more than just a great teacher, reformer, or prophet?
- What is the significance of Jesus being Jewish?

WRAPPING UP

Commit to an Act of Tikkun Olam

Read aloud the first two paragraphs of the section of chapter 4 titled "Healing the World" (page 95). Ask the group:

- What is the practice of tikkun olam?
- How can we practice "healing the world" in relation to the Jewish people in our community?

Distribute a blank index card to each participant. Ask them to pray silently, asking God to give them clarity about one act they could commit to do in the coming week that may lead to the healing of the world. Remind persons of the examples Hamilton lists in the passage you read aloud: caring for the sick and broken, feeding the hungry, clothing those in need, welcoming strangers, and visiting those in prison.

Invite participants to write down one commitment that they would undertake in the coming week.

After allowing some minutes for this activity, invite volunteers to share a commitment they have made. Do not force anyone to share.

Ask group members to take their card with them and place it in a place where they will see it each day, such as by their bathroom mirror.

Close with a Prayer

Close the session with the following prayer, or offer one of your own.

God, thank you for the richness of our faith that comes to us through the example of the Jewish people. Thank you for the Jewishness of Jesus and the earliest apostles. Thank you for our brothers and sisters who wake up every morning and say, "The Lord, our God, is one." Thank you for the way they seek to love their neighbor as they love themselves, and for the witness they show to us. Help us to be inspired by that witness as we seek to follow you. Help us to love you with everything that is within us, to love our neighbors, and to offer ourselves for the healing of the world. In your holy name. Amen.

5

ISLAM

PLANNING THE SESSION

Session Goals

As a result of conversations and activities connected with this session, group members should begin to:

- identify the historical roots and sacred texts of Islam;
- articulate some of the basic beliefs of Islam;
- understand connections between Judaism, Christianity, and Islam; and
- appreciate the possibilities and potential benefits of Muslim-Christian interactions.

Scriptural Foundation

To God Abraham said, "If only you would accept Ishmael!"

But God said, "No, your wife Sarah will give birth to a son for you, and you will name him Isaac. I will set up my covenant with him and with his descendants after him as an enduring covenant. As for Ishmael, I've heard your request. I will bless him and make him fertile and give him many, many descendants. He will be the ancestor of twelve tribal leaders, and I will make a great nation of him."

(Genesis 17:18-20)

49

Special Preparation

- Have Bibles available for those who may not bring them.
- Provide paper, pens, and pencils for participants.
- Arrange your seating in a circle or semicircle so that all participants can see one another.
- Provide a means for showing the DVD segment (e.g., TV/DVD player) and cue Session 5: Islam.
- Have additional sheets of blank paper available along with markers.
- Post one blank sheet of paper on the wall in a visible and accessible location.
- If you have access to a copy of the Quran in English, bring it to the session and place it on a table in the middle of your meeting space next to a Bible. Leave space on the table for the placement of five cardboard tubes (see below).
- On a large sheet of paper, draw two columns, one with the heading "Quran" and the other with the heading "Bible." Post the sheet in a visible and accessible place in your room.
- Collect five cardboard tubes (such as those found in paper towel rolls). On each one write one of the following words from the Five Pillars of Islam:
  1. Shahada
  2. Salat
  3. Zakat
  4. Sawm
  5. Hajj
- (If you do not have cardboard tubes available to you, you can substitute pieces of sturdy paper that are taped together to form a tube shape.)

GETTING STARTED

Opening Activity: Create a Word Cloud of Images of Islam

As participants arrive, ask each one to take a marker and write a word or phrase that he or she associates with Islam on the blank sheet of paper you posted before the session. Ask them not to write the words in a list, but in a more random "cloud" formation.

When everyone has arrived, direct attention to the word cloud you formed on the sheet. Ask:

- What images of Islam are reflected in this cloud?
- What other images would you add to the cloud? (Write these on the paper.)
- Are most of our images positive or negative?

Say to the group: "In his book, Adam Hamilton observes that many Christians didn't know much about Islam before the attacks of 9/11. He also makes clear how important it is for Christians to learn about the religion of Islam."
Ask:

- How has your awareness of Islam changed since the attacks of 9/11?
- Why do you think Islam is so important for Christians to learn about?
- What more do you want to know about Islam?
- How much do you interact with people who are Muslim?

Begin with Prayer

Pray the following prayer or one of your own:

God of Abraham and Sarah,
God of Isaac and Ishmael,
> *we want to love you with our soul, body, mind, and strength.*
> *We want to surrender our lives to your will and your work.*
As we seek to understand and love our Muslim neighbors more,
> *help us see in them a reflection of our own desire for you.*
Help us be the ambassadors for Christ
> *that you call us to be.*
In the strong name of Jesus, we pray. Amen.

LEARNING TOGETHER

Video Study and Discussion

In chapter 5, Adam Hamilton discusses Islam, recounting its origins, sacred text, and essential beliefs and practices. He also discusses ways in which Christians and Muslims differ and how we can understand images of violence in both Islamic and Christian texts. The chapter concludes with a call for us to be ambassadors for Christ with our Muslim neighbors. In the video, Hamilton recaps some of the major points of the chapter and includes parts of an interview he conducted with Sheikh Dahee Saeed. See a transcript of this interview on page 53 under the heading "Conversation with a Muslim."

Play the video segment for this chapter and then discuss some of the following questions:

- Adam Hamilton tells the story of Muhammad and uses several descriptions of him. What descriptions of Muhammad do you remember from the video? (Some of the descriptions are "honest," "searching for God," "a warrior.") What is something new that you learned about Muhammad?
- One of the areas of disagreement that Adam Hamilton notes concerns Jesus. Why is it important for Christians that Jesus actually died on the cross?
- How does Sheikh Saeed describe the importance of regular prayer in Islam? Why is it important to pray five times per day, at specific times? How would you describe the rhythm of prayer in Christian life and worship?
- During Adam Hamilton's conversation with the imam, the video showed scenes from the Islamic Center of Johnson County. What do you remember from those scenes? How does worship in the mosque differ from Christian worship? What looks similar?
- Adam Hamilton describes an encounter with a woman who was at the worship service where he talked about Islam. What was her reaction to the sermon? What does her reaction show about the importance of learning about and relating to our Muslim neighbors?

Book and Bible Study and Discussion

Present the Life of Muhammad in Four Acts

Divide the group into four smaller groups for this next exercise. Say to the group: "In the section of chapter 5 titled 'The Beginning of Islam: Muhammad,' Adam Hamilton describes the origins of the Muslim faith. Each of your groups is going to take one period from that story and present it to the class in whatever way you would like, the more creative the better.

CONVERSATION WITH A MUSLIM

The Islamic Center of Johnson County is the largest mosque in the greater Kansas City area. I asked one of the leaders, Sheikh Dahee Saeed, if he would explain to us the Five Pillars of Islam, the five fundamental practices and beliefs of a Muslim. Here's an excerpt of what he had to say.

We have five pillars that the Prophet Muhammad (peace be upon him) taught us. *Shahada* means to bear witness that there is no God but Allah—one God—and that his prophet is Prophet Muhammad (peace be upon him). The *Salat* is to pray five times every day. The first one is before the sun rises, and the last one is one hour and a half after the sun sets. Five times we have to start our day with thanking God and asking him for his help. And before we go to sleep we thank him for that beautiful day that he has given us. And we are thankful to you, O God, for a lot of blessings. Then we sleep. So we have to pray five times a day.

Zakat means charity. Every Muslim has to pay some money for the needy, the orphans, out of his money yearly. *Sawm*: We have to fast one month every year. It's called the month of Ramadan. Then the last pillar is *Hajj*. So we go on a pilgrimage to Arabia and visit the house of God. These are the five pillars of Islam.

I asked Sheikh Saeed if he could talk a little bit about ISIS and about the violence in the Quran. And here's what he said:

If ISIS are really Muslims, why they are killing Muslims? In the holy Quran, God said if you kill one person you going to get credited with bad deeds as if you killed all people [in the world]. And if you help someone to live, you're going to get a word from God as if you helped all the world. So if they are Muslims, why they are killing Muslims? That's it.

They are taking one verse—one verse that calls for killing people. But to understand the meaning of that verse, you have to read the whole page in the Quran. The same [is true] of the Torah. The same [is true] of the Bible. You cannot take just one line or two lines, and say, "Oh, this is from the Bible." No. You cannot do that. You have to read the whole thing.

53

You may use play-acting, drawing, a poem, or even pretend you are doing a news segment for the TV news."

Assign one of the following periods of the story to each group:

1. The setting—Mecca, Muhammad's early life before age twenty-five
2. Ages twenty-five to thirty-nine
3. Age forty to the move to Medina
4. From the migration to Medina to the spread of Islam

Ask the groups to skim the study book (pages 102–107) for information that they will need to prepare a creative presentation.

After several minutes, have each group present in the order above. Thank the presenters for their work. Then discuss:

- What new things did you learn in doing this presentation?
- What impressions do you have of Muhammad?
- What were the major themes of Muhammad's life?

Study Scripture Together

Say to the group: "One thing that Judaism, Christianity, and Islam all claim is a connection to Abraham as a common ancestor in the faith. Let's look at some of the passages related to Abraham and his children in the Bible. Note that these passages present a sometimes-disturbing picture of relations between Abraham, Sarah, and her servant, Hagar. Note also that Islamic tradition contains some other traditions about Abraham and his son, Ishmael."

Have participants get a Bible and divide into four small groups. Have each group take one of the following scriptures:

- Genesis 16
- Genesis 17:15-27
- Genesis 21:1-21
- Genesis 25:7-18

Have each group use the following questions to study their assigned passage:

- What does this passage tell us about Ishmael?
- What does this passage tell us about God's provision for Ishmael?

- How could this story have impacted the relationship between Isaac and Ishmael's descendants?

After some time for small group discussion, reconvene as a large group. Ask:

- In two sentences, what happened in the passage you were assigned?
- How would you describe Ishmael's place in God's story?
- How could these stories help people in the faith traditions that trace back to Abraham (Judaism, Christianity, and Islam) understand their relationship to one another?

Compare the Quran and the Bible

Say to the group: "In the book, Adam Hamilton talks about the importance of the Quran for the Muslim faith. In this next exercise we are going to look at differences between the Quran and the Bible and the way Christians and Muslims think about their sacred texts."

If you brought a copy of the Quran to the session, direct attention to it. Ask for a volunteer who will compare the Quran and the Bible while the rest of the class does this exercise. Have the volunteer look for differences in the size of the books, their structure, and their organization. Tell the volunteer you will ask for his or her observations at the end of the exercise.

Have the remaining members of the group turn to the section of chapter 5 titled "The Quran as God's Perfect Word" (pages 108–110). Ask them to skim the section looking for differences between the Quran and the Bible. Get a volunteer to go to the sheet with the words "Quran" and "Bible" that you posted before the session began. As participants call out differences they have noticed, have the volunteer write those differences in the appropriate columns.

Now have the group skim the section of chapter 5 titled "The Bible and the Quran" (pages 113–116). Repeat the exercise above, noting any new differences you find and recording them on the sheet.

If you have a volunteer looking at the Quran and Bible, invite the person to share his or her observations and record those on the sheet as well.

Discuss the following questions:

- How do you understand the major difference between how Muslims view the Quran and how Christians view the Bible?

- What does Hamilton mean by saying that Muslims view the word of God in light of the Quran and Christians through the lens of Jesus?

Explore the Five Pillars of Islam

Distribute the cardboard tubes (or alternatives), which you prepared before the session, to five volunteers. Ask participants to turn to the section of the book titled "The Five Pillars of Islam" (pages 110–112) and to keep a finger at that location. Ask them not to skim that section, but to rely on their memory for the next exercise.

In random order, have each of the volunteers hold up his or her tube and read (to the best of their ability) the word written on it. Acknowledge that it may be hard to pronounce the Arabic words. Ask the group to describe the Islamic practice to which this word refers. As the leader, you may use the book to indicate when the right answer is given. When the correct answer is given, place the corresponding tube on a table in the center of the group.

After all five tubes have been placed, ask:

- Which of these practices are also practices within Christianity?
- Which of these practices challenge you to live your Christian faith more deeply?
- Based on your experience, what are the essential practices of the Christian faith?
- What can Christians stand to learn about our own faith, or how can we grow in our faith, by paying attention to these pillars of Islam?

Discuss Violence and Sacred Texts

Ask group members to skim the section of chapter 5 titled "Islam and Violence" (pages 116–118). If you have time, read the section (or key parts of it) aloud. Discuss these questions:

- According to Hamilton, why do some Christians have the impression that Islam is a religion of violence?
- How does context help us understand violent passages in our sacred texts?
- How would you talk with someone about why a violent act done in the name of Christianity doesn't reflect the teaching of the Bible?
- How could we be good Samaritans for our Muslim neighbors?

WRAPPING UP

Write a Letter as an Ambassador

Read aloud the final paragraph of the section of chapter 5 titled "Christ's Ambassadors" (page 119), in which Adam Hamilton quotes 2 Corinthians 5:20 to talk about the importance of being ambassadors for Christ. Invite participants to reflect on what they might do personally to be an ambassador for Christ.

Distribute blank pieces of paper and writing instruments to members of the group. Invite group members to write a letter, either to an actual person of the Muslim faith whom they know or to an imagined Muslim acquaintance. Ask the group members to write a letter that reflects their honest desires to live with respect, kindness, and peace with the letter's intended recipient, including a reflection on how their personal faith informs their care for that person. Participants can determine whether or not they will send the letters.

If some persons find this exercise difficult, invite them to write the letter instead to God, offering God their thoughts and/or concerns.

After the exercise, ask:

- How difficult was this exercise?
- What did you learn about your own faith through writing this letter?
- What might you do as a next step?

Close with a Prayer

Close the session with the following prayer, or offer one of your own.

Loving God, we thank you for our Muslim neighbors, for the ideas and practices we share in common with them, and for the many ways we can learn from them to enrich our faith. Teach us to be Christ's ambassadors to them, embodying and witnessing to your love in the way we relate to all our neighbors of other faiths. We pray in the name of Jesus, who is your word made flesh. Amen.

6

CHRISTIANITY

PLANNING THE SESSION

Session Goals

As a result of conversations and activities connected with this session, group members should begin to:

- understand how Christianity answers humanity's deepest existential questions;
- appreciate John 3:16 as a summary of Christian beliefs;
- identify *chesed* and *agape* as biblical terms that illuminate God's character; and
- articulate an approach to other world religions from a Christian perspective.

Scriptural Foundation

> *For God so loved the world, that he gave his only begotten Son, that whosoever believeth in him should not perish, but have everlasting life.*
>
> *(John 3:16 KJV)*

Special Preparation

- Provide Bibles for those who may not bring them.
- Have paper, pens, and pencils available for participants.

- Arrange your seating in a circle or semicircle so that all participants can see one another.
- Provide a means for showing the DVD segment (e.g., TV/DVD player) and cue Session 6: Christianity.
- Post four sheets of paper on the wall, each titled with the name of one of the world religions we have studied: Hinduism, Buddhism, Judaism, and Islam.
- Have additional sheets of blank paper available along with markers.
- Prepare four cards, preferably on 8.5" × 11" (or larger) card stock, but on paper if necessary. On each card print one of the following phrases from John 3:16 in large, bold lettering:
  ◊ For God so loved the world
  ◊ that he gave his only begotten Son
  ◊ that whosoever believeth in him should not perish
  ◊ but have everlasting life
- Post a blank sheet of paper on the wall in a visible and accessible location.
- Have available tape or other adhesive to attach cards to the blank sheet of paper.

GETTING STARTED

Opening Activity: Do a Review of World Religions

After everyone has arrived, say to the group: "In this study, we have been looking at major world religions from a Christian perspective and trying to understand how they answer some of humanity's most basic questions about life and the universe. Today we will be studying our own faith—Christianity. Because this is our last session, however, let's do a little review of what we've learned so far."

Direct the group's attention to the four sheets you posted before the class began with the titles of the four world religions you have studied. Ask a volunteer to write responses to the following questions that you will ask about each of the religions. Ask:

- What are the sacred texts for each of these religions?
- What are the major beliefs of each?
- What else do you recall about these religions?

59

As group members answer the questions for each religion, have the volunteer write responses on the appropriate sheet. Use the study book to find answers if you get stuck. After spending some time filling in the sheets, discuss the following questions:

- What have you appreciated about studying world religions this way?
- What more do you want to know?

Begin with Prayer

Offer the following prayer or one of your own:

God, you are greater than our understanding
and higher than our highest thoughts.
Along with our neighbors,
we seek answers for the lives we live
and the things we do not understand.
We thank you for your revelation of yourself in Jesus Christ
and for his message of unending love.
It is because you loved us
that we seek to love others. Amen.

LEARNING TOGETHER

Video Study and Discussion

In chapter 6, Adam Hamilton turns to Christianity and examines it using some of the same questions he has used in looking at other religions. In the video, Hamilton summarizes the Christian faith using the lens of a very familiar verse: John 3:16. Breaking the verse down into four segments, he explores what God is like, how God's revelation in Jesus reveals the purpose of human life, how God offers forgiveness for sin, and what the Resurrection shows about the source of our hope. He concludes with a reflection on what he appreciates about other religions and why he remains committed to being a Christian.

Play the video segment for this chapter and then discuss some of the following questions:

- Adam Hamilton chooses John 3:16 as a summary of the gospel. Why is this verse so useful in helping us understand the basics of the Christian faith?

- Hamilton says that there are four basic questions that human beings ask. How many of them can you remember? (1. Am I loved? 2. Is there a purpose to life? 3. Can I be forgiven? 4. And is there hope?) How do we confront these questions in our lives?
- Near the end of the video, Adam Hamilton notes things that he can say yes to in all of the other religions we have studied. Why does he feel Christianity offers a fullness not found in the other religions?

Book and Bible Study and Discussion

Get to Know John 3:16

Say to the group: "Since John 3:16 plays such a prominent role in this chapter, we are going to get to know it very well. Let's begin with an exercise to help us remember what it says."

Invite four volunteers to come and stand in a line facing the rest of the group. Mix up the four cards that you prepared before the session and give one to each person. Using the cards as a guide, have them arrange themselves moving left to right (from the group's perspective) so that the verse is in the correct order. Now have the group read the verse aloud in unison.

Next, have the volunteers flip the cards over so that the words are not showing. Have the group recite from memory the first phrase of the verse. When the group has said the phrase correctly, have the first volunteer flip the card over. Repeat with the other phrases.

One last time, have the volunteers flip the cards over to the blank side and have the whole group recite the verse from memory. Then flip the cards over again.

Ask the volunteers with the second, third, and fourth phrases to keep the cards and sit down. Meanwhile, affix tape to the back of the first card and have the first volunteer place it on the blank sheet of paper you posted before the session began.

Explore Chesed and Agape

Say to the group: "This first phrase of John 3:16—'God so loved the world,' tells us something important about God's character—God is defined by love. The Bible uses two words to help us understand that love—the Hebrew word *chesed* and the Greek word *agape*. Let's explore how these words are used in the Bible."

Divide into two smaller groups, one studying the word *chesed* and the other studying *agape*. Have each group look up the following Scripture verses to explore how the words are used, noting that *chesed* is often translated as "mercy," "steadfast love," or "loving-kindness" and *agape* can be variously translated as well as a form of the word *love*.

Verses related to *chesed*:
- Numbers 14:19
- Psalm 23:6
- Psalm 103:8

Verses related to *agape*:
- Matthew 5:43-46
- Matthew 22:37-39
- 1 John 4:7-10

Ask the groups to consider how the Scripture passages help them understand the word they are studying, and how the word they are studying helps to define love. Then ask them to come up with a definition for the word.

Come back together as a large group and share your definitions. Discuss the following questions:

- How do these words help us understand the nature of God's love?
- How is this different from how we usually use the word *love*?

Consider How Jesus Reveals Our Purpose

Have the volunteer who has the card with the second phrase ("that he gave his only begotten Son") post his or her card on the blank sheet of paper beside or below the first phrase. Invite the group to read the second phrase aloud.

Discuss the following questions together:

- How does the second phrase of John 3:16 explain how "God so loved the world"?
- Hamilton calls Jesus "God's love letter in human flesh." What does God tell us in this love letter?

Skim or read aloud the section of chapter 6 titled "Jesus Loves Me, This I Know" (pages 134–135). Ask:

- According to Hamilton, what is the purpose to human life as revealed in Jesus?
- How does your community of faith offer love in action?
- As you look at the community you live in, who needs love right now? How could you show love in action?

Draw a Work of Art

Have the volunteer who has the card with the third phrase ("that whosoever believeth in him should not perish") post his or her card on the blank sheet of paper beside or below the second phrase. Invite the group to read the third phrase aloud.

Distribute two blank sheets of paper to each group member. Say to the group: "The third phrase of John 3:16 reminds us that we and the world are broken. Christians understand that this brokenness is a result of sin. Jesus comes to show God's love by redeeming us from sin."

Discuss the following questions together:

- Hamilton describes sin as "missing the mark." How does this help you understand what sin is?
- Why do we have difficulty talking about sin?

Ask the group to draw a picture on one of the pieces of paper you distributed. This picture should depict something in their lives or in the world that has been disfigured by the effects of sin. Assure participants that they will not have to share this picture unless they would like to.

After allowing some time for this exercise, say to the group: "Chapter 6 quotes Ephesians, which says that 'we are God's accomplishment'" (2:10). Adam Hamilton says the Greek root of the word accomplishment suggests that we are God's work of art or poetry, created to reflect God's love."

Ask the group to use their second piece of paper to draw the same subject they drew in the first drawing. This time, however, draw a vision of what God could do to transform that area of their life or of the world into a work of art. Invite volunteers to share their drawings as they wish, but do not pressure anyone to share.

Envision Eternal Life

Have the volunteer who has the card with the last phrase ("but have everlasting life") post his or her card on the blank sheet of paper beside or below the third phrase. Invite the group to read the last phrase aloud.

Direct the group's attention to the sections of chapter 6 titled "But What About Heaven?" and "Heaven on Earth" (pages 142–144). Ask the group:

- What images have you had of what heaven is like?
- What does it mean that we can start experiencing everlasting life now?
- How does this vision of everlasting life differ from some of the beliefs about the afterlife we have studied in other religions?

WRAPPING UP

Dance with Stella

Read aloud the section of chapter 6 titled "Learning from Love" (pages 144–145). Ask group members to consider when they have had a feeling like Adam Hamilton shared with his granddaughter, Stella. Ask:

- What can our experiences of love tell us about God's love for us?
- Who can you "dance" with this week, to experience and share God's love?

Give Thanks for Learning

Since this is the last session, invite group members to reflect on what they have learned and what they hope for. Ask the group to share their reflections in a brief form by stating what they are grateful for and what they hope for. Model this by beginning the sharing yourself.

Use the form: "I am grateful for…, I hope for…" Ask the group to proceed around the circle, beginning with the person to your right. If a person would rather not share, ask them to say, "Pass," and proceed to the next person.

When everyone has had a chance to share, proceed to the prayer.

Close with a Prayer

Close the session with the following prayer, or offer one of your own.

Thank you, God, for loving me. I accept your love. Help me to love you in return. Help me better to love my neighbors of other faiths. Jesus, I trust in you. Thank you for your life, for your teachings, for your death and resurrection. I accept your salvation. Forgive me, I pray, and help me to follow you. Holy Spirit, come and dwell in me. Form me, shape me, and help me to live a life of love. Amen.